KOALAS

Rob Waring, *Series Editor*

HEINLE
CENGAGE Learning

Australia • Brazil • Japan • Korea • Mexico • Singapore • Spain • United Kingdom • United States

Words to Know

This story is set in Australia. It takes place in the eastern area of the country, in and around the city of Brisbane [brɪzbən, -beɪn], Queensland.

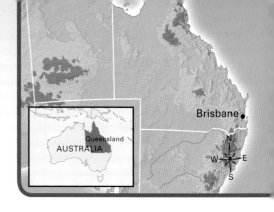

 Koalas. Read the paragraph. Then complete the sentences with the correct forms of the underlined words.

Koalas are a species of animal that lives in eastern and southeastern Australia. Koalas are not bears; they are a type of mammal called a 'marsupial' and have pockets on their stomachs in which the mothers carry their young. These furry animals survive entirely on a diet of eucalyptus leaves. In fact, eucalyptus forests are the koala's prime habitat, providing both food and water for the animal. The loss of these forests has recently made the koala vulnerable to the possibility of becoming endangered.

1. Most plants or animals live and feed in a specific _____.
2. Several plants and animals are _____ to the dangers that humankind causes.
3. _____ leaves are the main part of the koala's diet.
4. There are several different _____ of animals that live in Australia.
5. Cats, dogs and people, all of which have warm blood and bear live young, are examples of _____.

> ### Koala Facts
> - Koalas rarely drink water because they absorb their water from eucalyptus leaves.
> - Koalas sleep approximately 75% of the time, getting up around sunset to look for food.
> - Except for mothers and their young, mature koalas live most of their lives alone, not in large groups.

B Saving a Species.

Read the paragraph. Then match each word with the correct definition.

Over the last 200 years, the eucalyptus forests of Australia have been nearly decimated. The clearing of forests to build houses and roads has inevitably resulted in loss of habitat for the koala, which lives in the forest canopy. Luckily, members of the Australian Koala Foundation and their international colleagues are now working to ensure the animal's survival. They are developing legislation that limits what private landowners can do with their land. Other supporters are creating sanctuaries where koalas can live and be observed in their natural habitat.

1. decimate _____ **a.** a person who owns land

2. canopy _____ **b.** a safe, protected place

3. colleague _____ **c.** destroy; ruin completely

4. legislation _____ **d.** a proposed or passed law or set of laws

5. landowner _____ **e.** the area of a forest at the top of the trees

6. sanctuary _____ **f.** a person with whom one works

A Koala in a Eucalyptus Tree

The koala is so universally popular that it has become a kind of symbol for the country of Australia as well as being a very well-known – and loved – animal around the world. But what is it about koalas that attracts so many people, both young and old? The main factor seems to be the fact that koalas are just so incredibly cute! 'They're nice and furry and **cuddly**,'[1] says one koala-lover visiting a koala exhibit. 'They look like toys,' says another tourist from abroad. It's certainly easy to agree with these opinions when one looks at the furry grey animals sitting on tree branches, slowly eating eucalyptus leaves. The animals appear to be unbelievably relaxed and usually spend most of their time sleeping in order to conserve their energy.

When Europeans first saw koalas, they thought they resembled bears, and some actually believed they were bears. However, these small creatures are not a species of bear, but rather a type of mammal, called a 'marsupial,' and have stomach pockets in which mothers carry their young. Bear or not, the koala is truly one of the world's favourite animals. Another visitor to the koala exhibit may sum it up best when he says, 'I would **be hard put**[2] to find another mammal that is so recognisable internationally and so **beloved**.'[3] Unfortunately, while koalas may be cute and well-liked, love alone, the experts say, may not be enough to ensure the koala's future.

---

[1] **cuddle:** hug; hold gently and close
[2] **be hard put:** *(slang)* find it difficult to do something
[3] **beloved:** highly loved

Skim for Gist

Read through the entire book quickly to answer the questions.

1. What is the book basically about?

2. What are the main factors affecting the koalas?

Deborah Tabart is the **executive director**[4] for the Australian Koala Foundation and is also an expert on koalas. According to Tabart, the koala's survival prospects are not looking very good. 'I can tell you that I believe the koala's future in this country is **bleak**,[5] very bleak,' she says. The noise of the heavy machines clearing the forests on a local building site seems to reinforce Tabart's prediction. The development of natural areas in order to make residential and industrial buildings is big business in Australia and around the world. The eucalyptus forests that have always been home to koalas are being increasingly claimed and cleared for housing, farms and roads. This means that the koalas' habitat in eastern Australia is being radically reduced in some areas – some would even say decimated. The price of progress for human beings seems to be the koalas' habitat.

According to Tabart, each tree that is lost or cut down adds more pressure to the already vulnerable state of these animals. Australia has only been settled by people of European background for less than 225 years, but in that time an enormous amount of damage has been done to the natural habitat of these animals. As she walks into a eucalyptus forest, Tabart explains: 'Well, this is exactly the sort of habitat that used to be all over Australia. This is prime koala habitat and in the last two hundred years since we've been here, we've cleared about eighty percent of this.'

---

[4]**executive director:** the person responsible for the administration of a business
[5]**bleak:** with little or no hope

It seems, then, that a huge percentage of koala habitat has been eliminated, but that's not the sole difficulty facing the cuddly, furry mammal. The other issue is that the severely reduced koala habitat that remains is not adequately protected by national legislation. While there are some laws protecting koalas, Tabert would say those laws don't do enough. 'Eighty per cent of the koalas in Australia now live on private land,' she says, 'so there is absolutely nothing that says that you and I just really can't cut those trees down.'

The Australian Koala Foundation is responding to this problem by advocating for a National Koala Act. The act, which will effectively protect the remaining eucalyptus forests by law, includes **incentives**[6] for private landowners to help save the koala. Some consider changes to the legal infrastructure such as this to be the way of the future. It may virtually be the only way that one can ensure the survival of some of the world's threatened and endangered species.

---

[6]**incentive:** something that makes someone work harder; motivation

Tabart talks about the potential legislation and what it means for Australia. She reports that it's a matter of establishing a piece of legislation that will intervene in the decimation of habitat and provide benefits for the future. However, it must also be one that doesn't deny landowners too much and creates a conservation-friendly understanding about land use. Tabart explains: '[We need] to have a **visionary**[7] piece of legislation that says, "Look, this is the way it is. We're not telling you that you can't do everything. But if you want something for future generations, you're going to have to make some **concessions**[8] because you can't keep doing it the way it is."'

Tabart often speaks with conservationists, government representatives and lawyers on behalf of the Koala Foundation. She attempts to convince them that, contrary to popular belief, koala legislation does not need to be complex; there's no need for complicated documents that exploit landowners or set governmental limits on land use. She feels that they need a comprehensive habitat protection programme, but one that will accommodate landowners' needs. In her opinion, a few paradigm shifts regarding conservation as well as revisions to legislation could prove to be the solution. But while plans and ideas for the National Koala Act may be submitted in meetings, they are inspired in the forests. By taking groups of conservationists through the forests, Tabart is able to show them exactly what might be lost. 'Now this is a spot where koalas usually love. There [are] some lovely habitat trees just here,' she explains to one group as they walk through the forest.

---

[7]**visionary:** imaginative; far-seeing
[8]**concession:** something that is permitted or given to solve a disagreement

Identify Cause and Effect

Circle the cause and underline the effect in each of the sentences.

1. Once the legislation is put in place, it is hoped that it will ensure the future of the koala.

2. The landowners will have to make some concessions so that future generations can enjoy the koala.

3. In order to get inspiration for ideas, a group of conservationists goes into the eucalyptus forests.

The appeal of the koala – and the need to help save its habitat – even seems to reach overseas. American conservation lawyers and scientists have come to Australia to share their experience in helping to save habitats with their Australian colleagues. The United States and Australia may be on opposite sides of the globe, but people such as Mark Shaffer from a group called Defenders of Wildlife in Washington, D.C., have a common desire: they want to save threatened and endangered species.

The Defenders of Wildlife are all too familiar with the troubles and concerns that arise from the **clearing of land**[9] and the increased development of natural areas. Shaffer explains why he has come. 'I think we're really here to share our experience,' he says. 'I mean, the United States has had a long, long history of its own land-clearing, settlement, and development. And we've got about twelve hundred of our own species on our threatened and endangered species list.'

---

[9]**clear land:** remove trees and other natural ground cover to make land ready for development or other uses

As the group of lawyers and conservation scientists walk deep into the forest, it's easy to see how their shared love of nature brings them together. Although the views along the Australian coast are amazingly beautiful, they've not come here to look at the sea. Everyone in the group is looking up to the forest canopy, hoping to catch sight of a koala. 'There's one!' says one member of the group excitedly as she smiles, looking up at the grey ball of fur sitting sleepily in a tree.

Part of the appeal for the group when they're looking for koalas is actually being able to find them in the thick forests of eucalyptus. Val Thompson of the San Diego Zoo explains how to spot a koala. 'I wouldn't say they're easy to spot,' she says, 'but you know, once you have a certain search image, it makes it a little easier.' She then adds, 'But they're pretty good at being **camouflaged**.'[10] Thompson also points out that the koalas seem to be somewhat funny and shy too. She explains, 'The funniest thing is once you find them, they kind of try to hide their faces because I think they're thinking if they can't see you, you can't see them.'

---

[10] **camouflage:** a way of hiding something by making it look like its surroundings

While Koalas may be thought of as cute by almost everyone, they're more than just a so-called 'pretty face,' especially when considering Australia's economy. According to data from a study conducted on behalf of the Australian Koala Foundation, koalas generate a half a billion U.S. dollars in revenue for Australia every year through tourism and marketing, thereby contributing significantly to the country's economy.

Some theorise that one way to save the koala may be to combine tourism and conservation. This has been successfully done at the Lone Pine Koala Sanctuary in Brisbane, to the obvious delight of its visitors. The sanctuary has managed to create an environment that gives visitors a chance to see koalas up close while creating revenue that helps to save them. Tourists who come to Lone Pine not only get a chance to see koalas, they can also get a chance to cuddle one! For foreign tourists who have never had the chance to be so close to a koala, the opportunity can be irresistible. As they take tours and listen to lectures about the koala, one can see the intense interest in their eyes. Then finally, they get their big chance when one of the sanctuary employees announces, 'Welcome to Lone Pine. Do you want to come through and hold my koala?' The visitors can later have their picture taken with one of the beautiful little creatures.

Ensuring the future of the koala is an important task for the country of Australia. The Australian Koala Foundation estimates that the koala population has declined from at least 10 million koalas over 200 years ago to no more than 100,000 koalas in recent times. This rapid decrease in koala population is one of the primary reasons why the Foundation is so determined to make the National Koala Act a reality.

Luckily, it seems that the cuteness of the koala might be the factor that saves it in the end. For some, the appeal of such a cute and cuddly little animal could motivate them to make the changes needed in order to save it. However, if the thought of losing such a creature doesn't give people the incentive to help it, saving the koalas could be a cause for lost hope. After her visit to the Lone Pine Koala Sanctuary, Val Thompson makes a point when she says, 'I think the world without the koala would be a bit sad, because if you can't save the koala, who can you save?'

After You Read

1. What is the writer implying by calling the koala 'universally popular'?
A. The koala is genetically related to aliens.
B. Koalas are unique Australian animals.
C. The koala occasionally interacts with other Australian animals.
D. Koalas are found to be cute by almost everyone.

2. On page 4 which of these statements best expresses the opinion of the last tourist?
A. The koala is one of the most popular animals in the world.
B. Koalas are better than any other animal in Australia.
C. People all over the world want to protect koalas.
D. Koalas are well known because they look like bears.

3. Which of the following is contributing to the decimation of the koala's natural habitat?
A. the use of cars
B. housing development
C. illness in Koalas
D. a paradigm shift

4. The word 'sole' on page 8 can be replaced by:
A. single
B. somewhat
C. prior
D. arbitrary

5. To help protect koalas, the National Koala Act plans to:
A. arrest people who build homes
B. ensure more zoos will be built
C. educate landowners about koalas
D. offer some benefits to citizens

6. In paragraph 1 on page 10, 'it' in 'doing it' refers to:
A. destroying land
B. killing koalas
C. making concessions
D. creating future benefits

7. Which of the following is one reason that the group of conservationists go for a walk in the forest?
   A. to see eucalyptus trees
   B. to take photos of the sea
   C. to meet home owners
   D. to watch koalas in the wild

8. Why do some Americans join the meeting?
   A. because they know more about koalas than the Australians
   B. because they have had similar conservation issues
   C. because they want to study more about eucalyptus trees
   D. because they want to create a koala habitat

9. Val Thompson implies that koalas:
   A. have a sense of humour
   B. don't like humans
   C. are entertaining
   D. cannot see very far in the distance

10. Combining tourism and conservation might help the legislation because it will show that koalas can:
   A. survive in sanctuaries
   B. behave well near humans
   C. be good pets
   D. contribute to the national economy

11. What conclusion does Val Thompson draw on page 18?
   A. If koalas aren't saved, no endangered animal will be.
   B. The koala's habitat is easy to restore.
   C. Only popular animals will survive in Australia.
   D. The decimation of koalas will continue.

12. What is the main purpose of this story?
   A. to minimise the seriousness of the koala conservation problem
   B. to educate people about a specific conservation issue
   C. to argue that countries must pass legislation to protect nature
   D. to demonstrate the critical bond between plants and animals

HEINLE Times

HOMES FOR HUMANS
A SANCTUARY FOR KOALAS

New South Wales, March 8

Koalas, with their cute, expressive faces and gentle behaviour, are a favourite of animal-lovers all over the world. They exist only in Australia, and in the early 1900s, a demand for coats made from the soft, grey fur of these animals threatened to destroy the entire species. In the 1930s the Australian government passed legislation to protect the animals, but that didn't solve the problem. Since then, the clearing of land for development has displaced large numbers of koalas and resulted in an even greater threat to the survival of the species.

Luckily, as urban development continues to spread, some Australian construction companies are trying to find ways to balance the issues. They are working to create new housing for humans, while giving priority to protecting the habitat of the koalas. The developers of Koala Beach Estates on the north coast of New South Wales have managed to do just that. They've been able to follow the dictates of an ecologically sensitive building programme, while also providing an attractive living environment for people.

Work on the project began in 1993 with a thorough survey of the local koala population. First, a researcher for the Australian Koala Foundation fitted koalas in the area with radio transmitters. The information gathered by the researcher showed which koalas were permanent residents and which were visitors, and also which areas of the proposed development – even

Koala Populations of Australian States and Territories

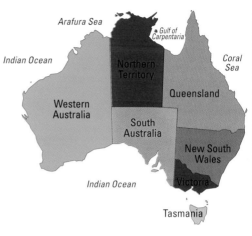

State	Estimated Koala Population*
Queensland	50,000
Victoria	20,000
South Australia	20,000
New South Wales	15,000

* data compiled from various sources

which specific trees – were used by the koalas. As a result of this study, the entire housing development was designed around the koalas' habitats.

Other koala-friendly components were included at Koala Beach Estates. Dogs and cats were banned from the development because they sometimes kill koalas. Planners also provided 'traffic calming' elements such as speed prevention methods and warning signs to protect the animals from cars. Since koalas have favourite paths between food trees, all fences were raised 30 centimetres above the ground to allow them to pass easily underneath.

Ropes were placed in swimming pools so koalas could climb out if they fell in. An enormous amount of careful planning went into the project, which resulted in a pleasant coincidence; twenty-five other rare or endangered species including bats, frogs and birds ultimately chose Koala Beach as their home. This bonus has increased homeowners' excitement over this outstanding wildlife-friendly community even more than expected.

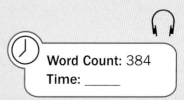

Word Count: 384
Time: _____

Vocabulary List

be hard put (4)
beloved (4)
bleak (7)
camouflage (14)
canopy (3, 14)
clear land (13)
colleague (3, 13)
concession (10, 11)
cuddle (4, 17, 18)
decimate (3, 7, 10)
eucalyptus (2, 3, 4, 7, 8, 11, 14)
executive director (7)
habitat (2, 3, 7, 8, 10, 13)
incentive (8, 18)
landowner (3, 8, 10, 11)
legislation (3, 8, 10, 11)
mammal (2, 4, 8)
sanctuary (3, 17, 18)
species (2, 3, 4, 8, 13)
visionary (10)
vulnerable (2, 7)